Sugar Reset and Cleanse Diet

The Ultimate Beginner's Sugar Reset & Cleanse Your System Diet Guide - 30-Day Natural Sugar Detox Plan, Lose Weight & Feel Great (Without Going Crazy & Fight Cravings!)

By *Isabella Evelyn*

For more great books, visit:

EffingoPublishing.com

Download another book for Free

We want to thank you for purchasing this book and offer you another book (just as long and valuable as this book), "Health & Fitness Mistakes You Don't Know You're Making," completely free.

Visit the link below to sign up and receive it:

www.effingopublishing.com/gift

In this book, we will break down the most common health & fitness mistakes, you are probably committing right now, and will reveal how you can quickly get in the best shape of your life!

In addition to this valuable gift, you will also have an opportunity to get our new books for free, enter giveaways, and receive other useful emails from us. Again, visit the link to sign up:

www.effingopublishing.com/gift

TABLE OF CONTENTS

Introduction 7

Chapter 1: What sugar does to your body .10

Chapter 2: Why do a Sugar Reset 20

Chapter 3: Benefits of doing a sugar reset and cleanse diet 28

Chapter 4: Prepping for your Sugar Reset 36

Chapter 5: What to expect in this 30-day Sugar Detox Plan 41

Chapter 6: How to do a 30-day sugar detox 46

Eliminate inflammatory foods 46

replacing trigger foods with anti-inflammatory foods 48

Breakfast Recipes 51

Pumpkin pancakes with vanilla bean coconut butter by The 21-Day sugar detox 51

Buffalo Chicken Breakfast Casserole 54

Sheet Pan Classic Breakfast Bake 56

Bacon Fat Deviled Eggs 59

Italian Sausage Frittata 61

Muffin-Tin Quiches with Smoked Cheddar and Potato 63

Crispy Turmeric Fried Egg 65

Lemon Poppy Seed Loaf by Clean Eating with Katie 66

Lunch Recipes **68**

Instant Pot Creamy Tomato Pesto Soup 68

Creamy Leek Soup Recipe 70

Paleo Clam Chowder 72

Easy Buffalo Wings.. 75

Mushroom, Spinach, and Sausage Crustless Quiche 77

Tuna Quinoa Salad in Endive Wraps 79

Slow-Cooker Vegetable Soup 81

Cauliflower Rice Stuffed Peppers 83

Dinner Recipes **87**

Sheet Pan Chicken with Sweet Potatoes Apples and Brussels Sprouts 87

Greek-Spiced Lamb Roast 90

6-Minute Salmon 92

Chimichurri Chicken Green Beans Skillet 94

Ginger Sesame Zucchini Noodles with Shrimp ...97

Carrot Meatballs with Mint Cauliflower Rice 99

No-Cook Black Bean Salad 102

Bang Bang Shrimp Lettuce Wraps 104

Snacks **106**

Toasted Pine Nut Herb Pumpkin Muffins 106

Granny Smith Apple Crumble 109

Vanilla "Milkshake" 111

Baked Eggplant Fries with Goat Cheese Dip 112

Savoury Almond Crackers 115

No-Bake Chocolate Banana Bites 118

Salt and Vinegar Popcorn Cauliflower 120

Garlic Aioli and Kale Chips 122

Sugar Detox Tips and Tricks **125**

Conclusion **131**

Final Words **133**

About the Co-Author **134**

Introduction

Do you know how much sugar you eat in a day? You might think it's not that much, but the truth is, we as a society are consuming far more sugar than we should be. Natural sugars, the kind found in fruits, vegetables, nuts, and dairy, aren't harmful. Processed sugars, however, promote a host of health problems that we often don't notice until it's too late.

Many chronic health problems are caused by unhealthy diets high in sugars and carbohydrates. Everything from obesity to heart disease to common fatigue can trace its origins, at least in part, to our diet. We must fix the systematic problems in our diets to reclaim our health and our lives.

This book aims to help you filter through biased misinformation to understand better how diets chronically high in sugar are harmful to you as well as how to conquer it. Remember to consult a doctor before making dramatic dietary changes, particularly if you have any preexisting health conditions, as changing your diet may add extra stress to your body.

First, we analyze the damages sugar does to your body. Sugary foods are known to promote tooth decay. The empty calories quickly lead to overeating and obesity, bringing with it an increased risk of high blood pressure, heart disease, cholesterol, chronic inflammation, and potentially even cancer.

Then we take you through the benefits of going through a sugar detox. You'll have more energy, notice clearer skin, and sleep better. Though you will likely experience sugar withdrawal, we take you through all the information and give you all the tricks to manage cravings so you can succeed at this sugar detox right from the get-go.

In this book, we provide everything you need to get started on your sugar detox journey. We'll help you reclaim your health and your life in just 30 days.

Also, before you get started, I recommend you joining our email newsletter to receive updates on any upcoming new book releases or promotions. You can sign up for free, and as a bonus, you will receive a gift. Our "*Health & Fitness Mistakes You Don't Know You're Making*" book! This book has been written to demystify, expose the top do's and don'ts and to finally equip you with the information you need to get in the best shape of your life. Due to the overwhelming amount of misinformation and lies told by magazines and self-proclaimed "gurus," it's becoming harder and harder to get reliable information to get in shape - as opposed to having to go through dozens of biased, unreliable, and untrustworthy sources to get your health & fitness information. Everything you need to help you has been broken down in this book for you to easily follow and to immediately get results to achieve your desired fitness goals in the shortest amount of time.

Once again, to join our free email newsletter and to receive a free copy of this valuable book, please visit the link and sign up now: www.effingopublishing.com/gift

Chapter 1: What sugar does to your body

We all know sugar as the sweet substance that makes your food taste more delicious. There's cane sugar, brown sugar, powdered sugar. All of those sugars fall into the processed sugars category. To explain better, let's begin at the cellular level.

Sugar is a simple carbohydrate that the human body stores as glucose, which can break down for energy. Once broken down into their simpler forms, all sugars are processed the same way. But before they reach that point is when sugars damage your body without you realizing.

The two main types of sugars are natural sugars and processed sugars. Natural sugars can be found in fruits, vegetables, and nuts. When eaten in moderate quantities in their natural form, sugars aren't inherently harmful to the human body. They're used as fuel to keep the body going. It's important to note, though, that sugars are not the only source of energy for our bodies. All the foods we consume are broken down to be used as energy. Sugars, particularly refined sugars, happen to be an easily processable energy source. Refined sugars, however, are often produced by food manufacturers chemically with the byproducts of sugarcane. Refined sugars are also used as fuel, but consumption of refined sugar comes with a host of health risks, and yet it makes up a surprisingly large part of our diet. Refined sugars are broken down quickly and provide little nutritional value. In other words, you'll keep snacking because you're still hungry despite that big meal you ate earlier (CTCA). They increase calorie consumption, interrupt your brain's processes, and interfere with many of your body's systems, leading to chronic illness. We must take steps to cut down our sugar intake to healthy levels to stop the progression of noncommunicable diseases and increase our quality of life.

We consume natural sugars through fruits, vegetables, dairy, and other sources, things that are natural parts of a healthy diet. Added sugars are... added. They don't occur naturally in the finished product, and these sugars are the ones that are particularly harmful to our health. This includes anything from adding natural sugars to a drink or the adding of chemically manufactured sugars during the industrial-scale production of food.

The modern diet is high in processed foods and refined sugars. The average American consumes over three times the amount of sugar recommended daily, and that has significant ramifications for our health. Various names for added sugars in products include brown sugar, corn sweetener, fruit juice concentrates, high-fructose corn syrup, and most molecules ending in -ose—dextrose, lactose, fructose, sucrose, and numerous others. That's not an exhaustive list. Avoid products with those words in the ingredients list, and keep in mind that if a food doesn't contain any fruits or nuts, all of the sugars in the product are added. Sugar-free and low-sugar labels mean that a product contains low levels of sugars per serving, but even foods with these labels contribute to the excess sugars in our diets (Sugar 101).

We expect that foods like chocolate and sodas are high in sugars, but how high are they? Chocolate contains an average of 62.6g of sugar per 100g of chocolate. That means chocolate is nearly 63% sugar. Soda contains 10.9g/100mL. Pop is almost 11% sugar. An average glass of wine can have as many calories as a slice of chocolate cake. Tomato ketchup contains a surprising 27.5g of sugar per 100 g. Even products like canned soups, salad dressings, and meat marinades contain added sugars (Top Sources of Added Sugar in Our Diet). All these added sugars add up quickly have a severe effect on our health.

Our first thought when we think of the dangers of consuming large amounts of sugar is dental health. Sugar is known for promoting tooth decay. And it's true. Sugar is a big part of the reason we get cavities in our teeth. The bacteria consume sugar in plaque, who use it as fuel the same way our bodies do, to produce an acid that attacks and destroys the protective enamel on the teeth. They eat away at the surface of the teeth, eventually leading to holes or cavities, and can even result in tooth removal. In England, cases of tooth decay in young children are on the rise, some having to get the majority of their baby teeth removed before the age of five. Research by WHO showed that the decay slowed when processed sugars made up less than 10% of the daily diet; however, keeping sugar consumption below 5% is believed to be the best course of action for your dental health (Sugars and Tooth Decay).

If rotting teeth isn't enough to scare you, another prominent side effect of consuming a high-sugar diet is an increased risk of obesity. Processed sugars contain high calories and few nutrients. They're digested quickly, leaving you feeling hungry, which leads to snacking, which leads to even more sugars in the body. These empty calories are absorbed rapidly into the bloodstream, leading to high blood sugar levels. Excess calories from sugar are stored in the body as fat, leading to rapid fat buildup. High blood sugar promotes insulin resistance, which in turn helps obesity. Obesity frequently leads to high blood pressure, putting you at risk of heart disease and strokes. But even if you exercise regularly to keep the fat off, you're still at risk of developing health problems because of your sugary diet (Kubala).

Several studies have shown an inverse correlation between dietary sugars and HDL cholesterol. The more sugar in the diet, the lower levels of HDL cholesterol. Low cholesterol sounds like a good thing, but there are different types of cholesterol. HDL "good" cholesterol works to take up LDL "bad" cholesterol, the one that causes health problems. Triglycerides are less talked about, but levels respond the same way LDL cholesterol levels do to a high-sugar diet. High levels of either Triglycerides and/or LDL cholesterol increase the risk of developing cardiovascular disease (Vascular Team).

High sugar consumption is known to lead to higher blood pressure and chronic inflammation, both of which are predecessors of cardiovascular disease. A 2014 study published by JAMA Internal Medicine identified an association between a high-sugar diet and a higher risk of death as a result of heart disease. Researchers followed subjects for 15 years and found that men who got between 17 and 21% of their calories from processed sugar had a 38% increase in their risk of death from heart disease than those who only consumed 8% of their calories from processed sugar. Cardiovascular disease, a condition involving narrowed blood vessels, can lead to heart attacks, strokes, and death (Harvard Health Publishing). Who knew that a piece of chocolate cake could cause a heart attack?

While research hasn't proven a direct link between sugary diets and cancer, there are numerous ways that sugary foods can contribute to our risk factors for cancer. Like the other cells in our bodies, cancer cells feed on glucose. Despite the popular misconception, however, eating sugars doesn't cause cancer to grow faster. Instead, the weight gain caused by empty calories increases your risk for thirteen different cancers, including breast, prostate, uterine, colorectal, and pancreatic cancers. And there may yet turn out to be a link between sugary diets and disease in other ways (CTCA).

One side effect that is certain about high sugar consumption is that it worsens inflammation. The body's natural inflammatory immune response to injuries is beneficial, but chronic diseases are thought to be the result of persistent inflammation over a long period. The natural reaction is inflammation and swelling in a localized area as a result of an injury. Still, the inflammation caused by high-sugar diets is a constant inflammation that can worsen joint pain and interfere with your body's natural immune response. This means that a diet that promotes unnatural levels of inflammation put you at risk of not only obesity and cardiovascular disease but also diabetes, nonalcoholic fatty liver disease, autoimmune disorders, and even mental disorders (Dimitratos).

On top of all of this, sugary diets have been linked to Alzheimer's disease. A study performed on mice showed that levels of inflammation in the brain rose more with a high-sugar diet than with a regular diet as the mice aged. Swelling in the hippocampus and the prefrontal cortex are traditionally associated with Alzheimer's disease, and a diet reminiscent of the one we eat every day promoted this (Savage). Do we want to continue to eat the way we're eating if it means we might one day forget even the names of our children?

Sugars make us feel right at the moment, but in the longer term, they leave us at risk for countless health problems. We haven't fully explored the damage sugar can do to our health here. Science hasn't either. What we do know is that sugar does more harm than good. There may be far more diseases caused by sugary diets that we haven't figured out are connected yet. Is it worth it to risk a lifetime of exhaustion, obesity, and general suffering to have the sweets we've become addicted to?

Chapter 2: Why do a Sugar Reset

We've established that sugars are harmful to you, so what can you do about it? You can do a sugar reset. Simply put, a sugar reset is a diet that cuts all sources of sugar out of your diet for a while. That means no harmful sugary desserts, no inflammatory sweetened beverages, and generally no processed foods. Instead, you'll eat wholesome, healthy meals prepared by you. By cutting out inflammatory foods and replacing them with healthier alternatives, you allow your body to heal from the damage caused by a chronically high-sugar diet.

The fact of the matter is that most people in developed countries, and even many who aren't, consume far more sugar than they should. Unless your diet is already nearly devoid of processed sugars, you could benefit from a sugar reset. If you find yourself going through your day, looking forward to chowing down on sweets at the end of it, or if you find yourself reaching for sweet snacks throughout the day, you could especially benefit from a sugar cleanse.

The sugar reset aims to rid your body of excess sugars and allows you to adapt to a more natural diet. Rather than reaching for addictive processed products, you'll find yourself reaching for healthier alternatives, and you'll enjoy their natural taste. We've established why sugar is harmful, so now let's take a look at the benefits of doing a sugar detox and creating a properly balanced diet.

Each day we're faced with countless options to choose from. Different flavors of one product, different brands with varying contents of calorie, fast food restaurants on every corner. When fatty, sugary foods aren't an option anymore, your complicated food options will become much more straightforward. Instead of asking yourself whether to eat in or out, whether to cook or prepare a frozen pizza in the oven, you'll expect yourself to cook a healthy, wholesome meal. You'll find your life in the kitchen greatly simplified.

Of course, you'll still have plenty of options with your meals. You just won't be overwhelmed by the possibilities anymore.

What's more, you'll be able to break free from the control of the food industry. With their artificial flavorings and added sugars, most of the food on supermarket shelves isn't right for you. Some people make living engineering food so that you quite literally become addicted. When you no longer feel addictive cravings to eat those unhealthy foods, you'll be free to make your own, informed choices about your diet and your health. You'll gain a better understanding of what makes your body feel good versus what gives you a dopamine rush that keeps you coming back.

Every choice you make ripples through your social network. It affects your spouse, your kids, your friends, your coworkers. In small ways, everyone is affected. When you take steps to cut sugar out of your diet, you're setting a positive example for all the people in your life who need it just as severely, if not more so, as you do. Chances are the people you interact with on a day to day basis are almost all suffering the same way you are at the hands of sugary foods. By being the first to try, you're laying down a path that others will follow. Wouldn't you love to encourage the people around you to live their healthiest, happiest lives? That can start with you. Be the example they need to take control of their life and their health. Teach your kids the value of a healthy diet and remind your coworkers what it feels like to wake up feeling rested and refreshed.

You won't only be working to better the lives of those close to you; you'll also be making a difference in the lives of the families who struggle to make a living harvesting sugar cane. They usually work under harsh conditions for low pay so they can provide for themselves and their families. By choosing to stop purchasing products laden with artificial sugars (produced from sugar cane), you're voting with your dollars to stop the inhumane treatment of sugar cane plant workers.

Processed foods are often produced in large factories and transported several times before reaching your hand at the store. Removing sugary products from your diet helps to cut out the industrial middle man. Mainly if you shop at open or farmers markets, you can be confident that the carbon emissions per unit of food are much lower than processed foods at the supermarket. The less processed the foods you buy are, the better for the environment they are too. Unfortunately, we can't say anything about how sustainably your produce was sourced, but consuming that produce, regardless, is a more environmentally friendly option than shipping that same product to a factory, processing it, and shipping it back.

We've focused a lot on how sugar affects people, but sugar also has far-reaching ramifications for the environment as well. The land has to be cleared to make room for sugar cane and sugar beet plantations. This destroys natural ecosystems and habitats. Heavy watering and the use of agrochemicals lead to polluted runoff that erodes the natural environment. Sugar cane, in particular, requires high amounts of water, leading to much more severe side effects from runoff. This is of more significant concern when you realize that up to 70% of artificial sugars come from sugar cane. This causes degradation of wildlife and all facets of the environment in areas connected to sugar plantations by waterways (Sugar and the Environment - Encouraging Better Management Practices in Sugar Production and Processing).

Healthy eating can indeed be more expensive than unhealthy food, but a large part of this conception comes from high prices of meats and superfoods. However, there are ways to tackle this. Buy frozen vegetables. They're cheaper than fresh, and since they're frozen soon after picking, they retain more of their nutrients than fresh vegetables. Many processed foods have a more affordable alternative, just waiting to be made in your kitchen. You can cook meals ranging from pasta sauces to loaves of bread, and the cost per serving can be lower than buying from the store. See Tips and Tricks at the end of chapter 6 for more ways to save eating healthy.

High sugar diets cause countless problems, not only for our health but for the environment and those forced to labor on plantations for low wages. Knowing this, it's hard not to understand the importance of reducing the sugar in your diet.

Chapter 3: Benefits of doing a sugar reset and cleanse diet

Naturally, when you cut out sugars, you'll be effectively working against the health dangers described in chapter one. You'll reduce your risk of obesity, heart disease, high cholesterol, and many more hazards we aren't familiar with yet. That alone is a significant improvement, but those aren't the only changes you'll notice. You'll feel more energetic, your skin will be healthier, and all around, your body will function more effectively.

On the surface, you'll notice improvements in your skin health. Sugary foods cause spikes in blood sugar, leading to a rise in insulin. When insulin spikes, oil production on the skin also spikes. Coupled with the increased inflammation, eating a high-sugar diet worsens acne. Research studies have demonstrated that lowering the amount of sugar in your diet can improve acne (Campos).

Sugar is also known to cause the cross-linking of collagen, one of the molecules that give skin its elasticity. Without its natural elasticity, damages to your skin show much more quickly. High-sugar diets emphasize the appearance of natural wrinkles in your skin. You might see more dramatic sagging in the skin on your neck and chin or the development of dark spots around your body. Cuts and scrapes may also heal slower as the skin's ability to repair itself is impaired (Unity point).

It's well documented that what we eat can impact our energy levels and our quality of sleep. Research has shown that high-sugar diets can stop our bodies from entering deep sleep, the kind of sleep our bodies need to heal and maintain healthy functioning. Sugar can also make it more difficult for you to fall asleep and can cause you to experience more restless night. Not to mention how sugar stimulates your appetite, which often leads to late-night snacking that only keeps you awake longer. Once you cut out sugar, you'll notice that you're not only sleeping better, but you have more energy during the day, too. A better night's sleep improves how you feel throughout the next day (Breus).

A miserable night's sleep can leave you feeling worse the next day, but sugar doesn't stop there. Sugar consumption is connected to depression. You heard, right. Higher levels of sugar consumption translate to a greater likelihood of developing depression. You might not have it, but continuing to eat a sugary diet and suffering daily from the chronic inflammation it causes put you at a much higher risk. Cutting out processed sugars can improve depression symptoms in those who have it and can lessen chances for those who don't (DiSalvo).

By cutting out sugar, you're cutting out a significant source of excess energy that often gets stored as fat. Without the excess energy floating around in your bloodstream, your body will have less to store as fat, effectively slowing, stopping, and even reversing fat buildup in your body. When you exercise, your body will begin to use up your fat stores, and you'll see them disappear. It's essential, of course, that you continue to eat a healthy amount of calories per day, but after removing sugary foods from your diet, you'll likely find it much easier to stick to a healthy number. Once you stop consuming excess calories, your fat buildup stops, and you'll be able to get rid of it much more quickly.

At one point or another, most of us have experienced eating a big meal and then feeling hungry again only an hour or so later. You can trace it back to what you stuffed yourself with. Sugars and simple carbs digest quickly, so you end up hungry again much quicker than when you eat complex carbs and proteins. After you cut unhealthy, sugary foods from your diet, you'll notice that you feel full much longer after meals and you don't feel the need to snack between them nearly as much as you did before (assuming you're eating three meals a day at regular intervals). Less urge to snack means less reason to chow down on sugars, which in turn means you aren't putting on as much fat. If you find that you do need a snack, however, check out the snack recipes provided in chapter six.

If you find yourself feeling bloated, sluggish, or weighed down, you may be suffering from excess water retention. When you consume lots of sugars, your body produces lots of insulin, which causes you to retain sodium, which leads to water being kept, rather than passed out of the body. In other words, sugars lead to your body retaining more water than otherwise necessary. The rapid weight loss at the beginning of a diet is often water weight as your body restores itself to a natural level of water retention. That's not to say that it's all water weight, or that losing water weight is a bad thing. In fact, losing excess water can make you feel better and more balanced (Greenfield).

Hormone imbalances, particularly in females, are known to cause irritability and moodiness, even contributing to anxiety and depression. On top of creating highs and lows energy-wise, sugar can disrupt your insulin levels, which in turn disrupts levels of estrogen and testosterone. Belly fat converts testosterone to even higher estrogen levels, putting the ratio of estrogen to progesterone even farther out of whack. This worsens moodiness and symptoms associated with monthly menstruation, and as women grow older, it can exacerbate the symptoms of menopause too. Cutting out sugars restores your body's natural balance of hormones. A healthy diet can dramatically reduce fatigue, moodiness, and even cravings, you may experience in conjunction with your monthly cycle (Arora).

A 1970s study showed that after consuming a large amount of sugar, your body's white blood cells are put at a temporary disadvantage and struggle to attack invading cells. While that's only one of many facets of the body's immune response, there hasn't been a lot of research into sugar's effect on the immune system. We know that it suppresses at least a portion of the immune response, and the state of inflammation it promotes further damages the body's ability to respond to threats. Your body's natural immune response is restored when you eat a healthy diet, leaving you healthier and happier in the long run (Reinagel).

Sugar affects the body in many ways, and cutting it out of your diet reverses those changes. Some of them you'll notice almost instantly, and some provide a lifetime of benefit. If all these positive changes occur when we cut out sugars, what are you waiting for? Hopefully, your answer is nothing, and you're ready to get set and dive in. Up next, we're discussing how to prepare for a sugar detox to set you up for success.

Chapter 4: Prepping for your Sugar Reset

Now, you might be asking yourself how you can do a sugar reset. The first thing to consider is preparing for your sugar cleanse. What can you do to set yourself up for success?

If you're not aware of how much sugar you're consuming, you should take steps to become informed. Start looking at labels to see how much sugar you're consuming and how much of it is artificial sugars. Begin keeping a food journal to keep track of how much sugar you're eating. Take note of when you snack and when you're most likely to be eating sugary foods. Are there any foods that you frequently eat that you shouldn't? Are there specific moods or situations that make you more likely to eat sugary foods? Once you understand what pushes you to eat unhealthily, you will be more prepared to address it.

Make meal plans. At the beginning of each week, sit down and plan out your meals for the coming days. Keep in mind what days you're busy and plan out more natural meals or things that you can prep beforehand for those days. Don't be afraid to throw new recipes into the mix.

Begin making shopping lists. Once you have a meal plan for the week, you can shop for the items that you'll need to prep those meals. If you have a specific list of things to buy, you'll be more likely to stick to that list rather than wandering the aisles looking at all the processed foods you're addicted to eating. Greasy, sugary foods are designed to be addictive. Chemical engineers make their careers by creating flavor profiles that make it nearly impossible to stop yourself from eating them. By making shopping lists and sticking to them, you eliminate the possibility of giving in and stocking your pantry with bags of chips and packages of cookies.

Clear out your pantry of harmful foods. Take stock of what snacks, instant meals, and other foods you have on hand. Chances are, you'll realize that you have a lot more food, more specifically a lot more unhealthy food than you thought you had. Throw out anything that's expired or that no one in your household eats. Get rid of unhealthy foods and commit to not repurchasing them.

Bring in healthy replacements. Instead of buying unhealthy foods, bring in more fruits, nuts, and vegetables. Pack kids' lunches with slices of celery, carrot sticks, or even bell peppers instead of cookies, and pack healthy sandwiches or leftovers from healthy meals. Finish what you have before buying new foods. Don't buy new packages of something unless you have no more at home. If you've finished an unhealthy product, bring home a healthier one to replace it.

Tell the world. You're going to succeed at a 30-day sugar detox, and the world wants to know about that. Tell the people you interact with daily what you're planning to do and ask for their help. Ask them to make sure healthier options are available when you're around. Ask them to slap you if they see you eyeing that donut. Ask them to join you. It's up to you! Some prefer posting on social media and giving daily updates on how they're doing. Others would prefer the support of a few close loved ones. You know what works for you. Do it. If a buddy to keep you on track would help, then find a buddy. If you'd prefer that your spouse hides all the sugary foods in the house, ask them to. You can totally succeed at this, and having the support of those around you will make it far easier to manage.

Look online. If you can't find support in person, look online. There are millions of people out there willing to support your endeavors; it just might take a bit of venturing outside your comfort zone to find them. Maybe you'll find a group that shares recipes and secrets about where to find the best produce. If so, fantastic. Perhaps you'll find a couple of people willing to check in on you each day. That's awesome too. Every person you have supporting you is someone you can talk to instead of giving in to the cravings when they come.

Chapter 5: What to Expect in This 30-Day Sugar Detox Plan

During this 30-day detox, you will cut out all processed sugars from your diet for 30 days. You will replace inflammatory foods with healthier alternatives and learn to manage stress and emotion in ways other than eating sugars. During the first week, you'll struggle with cravings and symptoms similar to those of caffeine withdrawal as your body responds to a lack of sugar. During the second week, your symptoms will most likely have subsided, but you'll still suffer from cravings. Week three is when you begin to experience the benefits of living a low-sugar lifestyle. And beyond the month, you should do your best to continue a low-sugar lifestyle. After these 30 days are up, you'll be convinced.

Plan out your meals beforehand, and get support from the people around you to best set yourself up for success. You can expect to experience a wide variety of things when you begin this 30-day sugar detox, both positive and negative. You can expect to experience new foods, have more energy, and unfortunately, you can expect sugar withdrawal.

Let's begin with the more positive expectations.

Without the rollercoaster of blood sugar levels, you'll notice that you're sleeping better almost immediately. Along with that comes more energy during the day.

You can expect to try new foods as you experiment to find new substitutes for your favourite foods. You'll eat new meals, combine new flavours, prepare foods differently. Cutting out processed foods means making significant dietary changes, and it's essential to find fresh foods to replace your regular staples. Who knows, you may even discover your new favourite meal.

As your tastebuds adjust from the highly palatable foods of a high-sugar diet, you can expect to taste foods differently. You'll become more sensitive to the natural tastes of foods. Fruits and nuts will start to eat sweet as your tastebuds forget the overly sweet tastes of highly processed foods.

Unfortunately, sugary foods are addictive. It's so hard to stop eating sugars because your brain is wired to be addicted to them. When you stop eating sugar, your brain responds the same way it would if you were to stop a drug or alcohol you were addicted to. It's not a matter of willpower to stop eating sugar. It takes dedication and hard work to overcome your sugar addiction.

When you stop eating sugars, you can expect to go through sugar withdrawal. Sugar withdrawal is a real thing, and when you begin this sugar detox, you can expect to be faced with it. Symptoms include cravings, headaches, fatigue, nausea, cramps, irritability, and feeling depressed. They should be mild and fade in time. As your body adjusts, these symptoms will subside in a few days or weeks, and you will begin to feel better than you did before. If you decide to cut down on sugar slowly, these symptoms will last longer, but they may be even milder than going cold turkey (Eske).

You can deal with sugar withdrawal in several ways. Magnesium is a molecule known for helping to reduce blood sugar levels and make protein, which can help regulate the symptoms of sugar withdrawal. You can get your daily recommended magnesium through servings of spinach, whole grains, milk, black beans, and peanuts. Other tips for managing sugar withdrawal are to eat protein to help control your appetite, to drink enough water, so you don't worsen or cause new headaches, and to exercise to help regulate your blood sugar levels (Eske).

If you begin to experience symptoms of hypoglycemia (extremely low blood sugar), including unusual dizziness, trouble concentrating, inability to eat, loss of consciousness, or seizures, contact a doctor (Eske).

Most importantly, expect that you will make mistakes here and there. If you go in expecting perfection, making a mistake will be very disheartening. The point of a sugar detox is to improve your health, but if you give up after a single mistake, you won't get very far. Be forgiving when you mess up and give in to cravings. Make a note of what led you to make a mistake and use it as a learning opportunity..

Chapter 6: How to do a 30-day Sugar Detox

Eliminate Inflammatory Foods

Remember, the goal of a sugar detox is to cleanse your body of excess sugars and allow it to adjust to a healthier, more natural diet. Your main goal is to eliminate processed sugars from your diet. Cutting out sugary foods gives your body a chance to heal from what's likely years of excess sugar consumption.

One significant contributor is eating out. Fast food restaurants are known for being unhealthy options, but people tend to choose them regardless out of convenience. Coupled with the health risks the greasy food brings, it's simply not an excellent choice to save a couple of minutes. Fast food should be the first thing to go. Eating out at non-fast food restaurants can be a nice change of pace, but it's challenging to keep track of where sweeteners may have been added between the farm and your plate.

Foods like cereals, too, contain large amounts of sugar. Most store-bought carbohydrate products contain added sugars, even though it might not taste like it. Our taste buds are so accustomed to eating sweet foods that even many savory options are sweetened. If you want to enjoy a slice of toast, it's much healthier to bake your bread—and it can be a great way to spend time with your family, too.

It goes without saying that cookies, candy, ice cream, cake, and many other dessert products also have to be cut. The critical point here is to remove as much manufactured food from your diet as possible. Make what you can from scratch and enjoy a nice meal at home rather than going out. Invite friends and extended family members over if you want to make it really special.

Some might prefer to cut out sugary foods by throwing them all away. Others would prefer to replace them as they go, consuming what's left of their inflammatory goods before replacing them with healthier alternatives. If you have a pressing health need, such as type two diabetes or heart disease, you'll experience the health benefits faster the faster you cut out sugars.

After you cut out inflammatory foods from your diet, you'll begin to experience the benefits of the sugar cleanse diet.

REPLACING TRIGGER FOODS WITH ANTI-INFLAMMATORY FOODS

To be successful in this 30-day sugar detox, you're going to need to replace your unhealthy eating habits with healthier ones. It's essential to know beforehand what your trigger foods are. What foods are the ones you crave most? What foods do you reward yourself by eating? What foods do you have trouble controlling yourself around? Those foods are going to be the hardest and most important to replace. So let's take a look at how to establish a healthier diet and replace your inflammatory trigger foods.

Sodas are one of the worst beverages for you because of their high sugar content. Not to mention, they're dehydrating. Even diet sodas aren't healthy options. They replace sugar with artificial sweeteners, leaving them with the same risks as non-diet sodas. Juices, too, have high sugar content. Even alcohol has more sugar than you'd expect. Replace sugary drinks with sparkling water or water with added fruits and vegetables (note: not juices, slices of fruit or vegetables).

It's not as simple as replacing sugar with natural, artificial sweeteners. Those artificial sweeteners trigger the same neurochemical rush that you get when you eat traditional sweets, and they have many of the same health risks. Instead, you have to find replacements that occur naturally.

Make sure you're hydrated. Any time you feel like snacking, drink a glass of water and then ask yourself if you still feel hungry. Don't forget to drink water throughout the day so your body is adequately hydrated.

Sugar cravings are going to be one of the hardest parts to conquer in this 30-day detox diet. Rather than filling yourself with empty calories, replace them with healthy fats. Fats digest slower than sugars and keep you feeling full longer. Your blood sugar levels will be more stable, preventing energy crashes that leave you craving sugar.

Healthy substitutes for sugary foods include avocado, nuts and seeds, coconut products, and more. Cook meals using these substitutes to keep yourself feeling full and satisfied.

Instead of snacking on cookies, chips, or other snacks, instead eat fruits or nuts. If you're craving something sweet, try apple slices or other healthy fruit options. Spice it up with unsweetened yogurt or peanut butter. If you're craving something a little more savory, try some lightly salted nuts. For dessert, have fruit instead of sweets, or try some of the snacks recipes in the snacks section below.

BREAKFAST RECIPES

Pumpkin pancakes with vanilla bean coconut butter by The 21-Day sugar detox

- 6 eggs

- 3/4 cup canned pumpkin

- 1 1/2 teaspoon pure vanilla extract

- 1 1/2 teaspoon pumpkin pie spice

- 1 1/2 teaspoon cinnamon

- 3 tablespoons coconut flour

- 1/4 teaspoon baking soda

- pinch of sea salt

- 3 tablespoons ghee or coconut oil

- For the vanilla bean coconut butter:

- 3 tablespoons coconut butter

- 3/4 teaspoon pure vanilla extract

- seeds from 1/2 of a vanilla bean pod

DIRECTIONS

- In a large mixing bowl, whisk the eggs, pumpkin, and vanilla. Sift the pumpkin pie spice, cinnamon, coconut flour, and baking soda, and salt into the wet ingredients. Alternative option: combine all ingredients in a food processor until well mixed.

- Grease the skillet with 1 teaspoon of ghee and spoon the batter into the skillet to make pancakes of your desired size. Allow the pancakes to cook for about three minutes, and when a few bubbles appear, flip the pancakes once to finish cooking for another three minutes.

- Serve with bacon or sausage.

- Combine the coconut butter, vanilla, and vanilla bean seeds in a small mixing bowl.

- Mix well to combine, then use it to top pancakes.

Buffalo Chicken Breakfast Casserole

- 8 eggs

- ½ cup full-fat coconut milk (I haven't tried it myself, but my readers have said that cashew or almond milk works great in place of the coconut milk!)

- ½ cup hot sauce (Tessemae's or Frank's Original work great)

- ½ teaspoon garlic powder

- 1 teaspoon of sea salt

- ¼ teaspoon black pepper

- 2 cups chicken, cooked and shredded (I used leftover rotisserie chicken)

- 2 scallions, chopped (approximately 1/3 cup)

- 1 cup spinach, chopped

DIRECTIONS

- Preheat your oven to 350 degrees. Lightly grease an 8x8" baking dish with coconut oil or ghee.

- Whisk the eggs in a large bowl. Whisk in the coconut milk, hot sauce, garlic powder, salt, and pepper. Add the chicken, scallions, and spinach, and stir well.

- Pour the egg mixture into the greased baking dish. Bake for 30-40 minutes, or until the center of the casserole is set. Cut into square slices and enjoy!

Sheet Pan Classic Breakfast Bake

- 2 large yellow potatoes, cleaned and diced to 1/2" cubes (see note)

- 1 medium onion, small dice

- 1 red or green bell pepper, small dice

- 1 teaspoon avocado oil (see note)

- 1/2 teaspoon garlic powder

- 1/2 teaspoon chili powder

- 1/2 teaspoon dried parsley

- 6 pieces nitrate-free bacon

- 4 pasture-raised eggs, more as desired

- fine sea salt and fresh ground pepper, to taste

DIRECTIONS

- Pre-heat oven to 400°F and line a rimmed baking sheet with parchment paper.

- In a large bowl, combine diced potato, bell pepper, onion, avocado oil, and spices. Toss to combine and pour onto a rimmed baking sheet.

- Place in the oven and bake for 20 minutes.

- Remove pan and move the vegetable mixture to one side of the pan. Add bacon in strips to the other side and return to the oven for 12 minutes.

- Remove from the oven and move bacon to the side. Move the hash brown mixture around with excess bacon fat to get the potatoes nice and crisp. Move potatoes back to the side and create four small divots in potatoes to crack the eggs. Crack eggs in the divots and return to the oven to bake for 8-10 minutes. Bake until eggs are cooked for the desired texture. 8 minutes are soft runny yellow yolks or 10 minutes for more fully baked eggs.

- Plate the hash browns and eggs on to a plate and briefly drain the bacon of excess fat on a paper towel before plating and serving. Put salt and pepper to taste (but taste it first as the bacon does add salt to the dish).

Bacon Fat Deviled Eggs

- 6 eggs

- 5 slices bacon, cooked and crumbled

- ¼ cup bacon fat (reserved from cooked bacon and still warm)

- ½ teaspoon garlic powder

- 1 teaspoon of sea salt

- ¼ teaspoon black pepper

- cayenne pepper (optional)

- 1 tablespoon chives minced

DIRECTIONS

- First up, let's hard-boil those eggs! My new favorite way to do this is actually to steam them, as I never have any issues with the shells sticking to the egg. Add approximately 2" of water to a pot. Bring to a boil. Add the cold eggs to a steamer basket in the pot, and steam, covered, for 9 minutes. Remove the eggs from the basket and immediately place them into a bowl filled with ice water. Allow the eggs to cool.

- Peel the eggs carefully, and cut them in half, lengthwise. Remove the yolks and place them into your food processor along with the warm bacon fat, garlic powder, sea salt, and black pepper. Puree until the mixture is smooth. No food processor? No problem! Mash the ingredients well, using a fork.

- Spoon the egg yolk mixture into the egg whites. Top with the crumbled bacon, chives, and a dash of cayenne pepper (if using).

Italian Sausage Frittata

- 1 tbsp coconut oil

- 1 lb Italian pork sausage (preferably pastured/organic, removed from the casings and crumbled, if necessary)

- ½ cup sundried tomatoes

- 1 cup spaghetti squash cooked (cooking instructions below)

- 3 garlic cloves, minced

- ½ tsp salt

- 8 eggs, beaten (preferably pastured)

- 1 tbsp chives, minced (optional)

DIRECTIONS

- Spaghetti Squash – Preheat your oven to 425 degrees. Cut the spaghetti squash in half, lengthwise. Place the squash face down on a baking sheet and bake for 20-30 minutes (depending on the size of your squash, this is for a small one) until the skin is soft and the threads of the squash come out quickly with a fork. Reserve 1 cup of squash for the frittata.

- Frittata – Preheat your Oven to 350 degrees

- Melt the coconut oil in an ovenproof skillet over medium heat. Once the oil has melted and the skillet is hot, crumble the Italian sausage into the pan. Cook for 3-4 minutes, or until it is no longer pink. Add the garlic to the pan and sauté until fragrant, about 30 seconds. Add the spaghetti squash to the pan and give it a good stir. Sprinkle the sun-dried tomatoes on top of the pork and squash. Add the eggs to the pan.

- Place the pan into the oven and bake for 15-20 minutes, or until the eggs are set. Enjoy!

Muffin-Tin Quiches with Smoked Cheddar and Potato

- 2 tablespoons extra-virgin olive oil

- 1½ cups finely diced red-skinned potatoes

- 1 cup diced red onion

- ¾ teaspoon salt, divided

- 8 large eggs

- 1 cup shredded smoked Cheddar cheese

- ½ cup low-fat milk

- ½ teaspoon ground black pepper

DIRECTIONS

- Preheat oven to 325 °F. Coat a 12-cup muffin tin with cooking spray. Heat oil in a large skillet over medium heat. Add potatoes, onion, and ¼ teaspoon salt and cook, stirring until the potatoes are just cooked through about 5 minutes. Remove from heat and let cool 5 minutes. Whisk eggs, cheese, milk, pepper, and the remaining ½ teaspoon salt in a large bowl. Stir in spinach and the potato mixture. Divide the quiche mixture among the prepared muffin cups. Bake until firm to the touch, about 25 minutes. Let stand 5 minutes before removing from the tin.

- To make ahead: Individually wrap in plastic and refrigerate for up to 3 days or freeze for up to 1 month. To reheat, remove plastic, wrap in a paper towel, and microwave on High for 30 to 60 seconds.

Crispy Turmeric Fried Egg

- 2 eggs

- 1 teaspoon turmeric or Further Food Turmeric Tonic

- ½ tablespoon ghee or avocado oil

DIRECTIONS

- Heat a cast-iron skillet on medium-high heat.

- Add ghee and turmeric, stirring as it melts to create a slurry.

- Crack the eggs into the slurry and immediately turn the heat to low.

- Cook until the whites are no longer runny.

Lemon Poppy Seed Loaf by Clean Eating with Katie

- ½ cup full-fat coconut milk
- 4 pasture-raised eggs
- 4 green-tipped bananas
- 1 2/3 cup almond flour
- zest of 4 lemons
- 2 lemons juiced
- 2 tsp. poppy seeds
- 1 tsp. vanilla
- ½ tsp. sea salt
- optional: ¼ cup coconut butter melted

DIRECTIONS

- Preheat oven to 325 degrees Fahrenheit. Grease a loaf pan with coconut oil and line with parchment paper.
- Combine the first four ingredients in a food processor and mix until combined. Then add the remaining ingredients and mix until just combined.

- Pour mixture into greased loaf pan. Cook for 65-70 minutes or until golden brown on top and loaf is firm when pressed in the center.

- Allow cooling for 20-25 minutes. Drizzle with melted coconut butter if desired.

Lunch Recipes

Instant Pot Creamy Tomato Pesto Soup

- 2 (28 ounces) cans of whole, peeled San Marzano tomatoes

- 1 (16 ounces) bag of frozen cauliflower

- 1 (32 ounces) container of chicken bone broth

- 3 tablespoons basil pesto (I used this dairy-free brand, but you can also make your own) plus extra for garnish

- 1-2 teaspoons salt (to taste)

- 1 teaspoon garlic powder

- 1 teaspoon dried oregano

- 1/2 teaspoon black pepper

- basil leaves, for garnish

DIRECTIONS

- Place all ingredients in an instant pot, secure the lid, close off the pressure valve and press the Soup button and press down to 15 minutes.

- Once it is done the cooking, release the pressure valve with a natural release or a quick release. Once you remove the lid, use an immersion blender to blend the soup until completely smooth. Taste to see if the soup needs any extra salt or pepper.

- Garnish the soup with extra basil extra and basil leaves!

Creamy Leek Soup Recipe

- 3 cups leeks dark green ends removed, roughly chopped (~2 medium leeks)

- 1 cauliflower medium, ~2 lb, chopped

- 1 onion medium chopped

- 4 cups chicken broth

- 1 tbsp ghee optional

- 1 cup coconut milk full fat

- Sea salt and black pepper to taste

DIRECTIONS

- Wash the leeks well. Cut off the root end, then slice it down the middle lengthwise. Hold under running water and separate the leaves, rinsing well...especially the outermost leaves. Sandy soup is not delicious. Cut off the dark green top and save them for making stock. Chop the leeks roughly. Add to a large soup pot.

- Cut the core out of the cauliflower and trim off any leaves. Roughly chop it. Add that to the pot.

- Add the onion, chicken broth, and ghee (optional) to the pot.

- Bring to a boil, then reduce to a simmer for about 20 minutes or until all the veggies are tender.

- Allow to cool slightly, then add the coconut milk. Puree the mixture until smooth using a blender. Caution: You may need to do two or more batches, so the blender doesn't overflow. Be careful when blending hot liquids.

- Season it with salt and pepper, to taste.

Paleo Clam Chowder

- 1 cup raw cashews

- ½ cup water (plus some additional water to soak the cashews)

- 2 tablespoons ghee or grass-fed butter

- 1 small yellow onion, finely diced

- 2 celery stalks, ends removed, finely diced

- 2 tablespoons arrowroot or tapioca starch

- 1 pound peeled and diced red potatoes

- 2 cups chicken broth

- 3 – 6.5-ounce cans of chopped clams, packed in juice

- 2 bay leaves

- Sea salt and pepper, to taste

DIRECTIONS

- Place the cashews in a clean bowl. Bring a small pot of water to a boil, and then pour the water over the cashews to soak. The cashews should be fully immersed in the water. Set aside.

- Melt the ghee/grass-fed butter in a medium-sized pot over medium heat. Add the onion and celery to the pan and sauté until soft, about 5 minutes. Stir in the arrowroot/tapioca starch until well combined.

- Add the potatoes, chicken broth, juice from the clams (don't add the clams just yet), and bay leave to the pot. Stir the mixture well and bring to a gentle boil. Reduce the heat and simmer for 15-20 minutes, or until the potatoes are fork-tender, stirring occasionally.

- Drain and rinse the cashews. Place the cashews in your blender, along with ½ cup of fresh water. Blend on high for 2 minutes, or until the cashew cream is smooth.

- Remove the bay leaves from the soup. Add the cashew cream along with the clams and stir well. Return to a simmer and cook for 2 minutes while stirring often. Season with salt and pepper to taste. Top with bacon and chives if you'd like.

Easy Buffalo Wings

- 6 chicken wings (6 wingettes, 6 drumettes)

- 1/2 cup Frank's Red Hot Sauce

- 2 tbsp butter

- salt

- pepper

- garlic powder

- paprika

- cayenne (optional)

DIRECTIONS

- Start by breaking your chicken wings into 2 pieces (the vignettes and drumettes, discarding the tips). Pour a bit of Frank's Red Hot sauce over the wings, just enough to coat them lightly.

- Season your wings and toss to cover them well. Refrigerate for about an hour. If you're strapped for time, you can skip the refrigeration and move on to the next step.

- Turn your grill on to high and place the oven rack about 6 inches from the broiler. Line a baking sheet with aluminum paper. Layout the chicken wings, so they have enough space between them for the flame to reach the sides.

- Let them cook under the broiler for about 8 minutes. The tops of the wings should turn a nice dark brown. Some bits may turn almost black if they're very close to the flames.

- While they're broiling, meltdown 2 tablespoons of butter and the rest of your hot sauce. You may season it lightly with cayenne pepper if you'd like a spicier wing as we do! Once the butter has melted, take the sauce off the heat.

- Take the wings out of the grill and flip them. Place them back in the broiler for 6-8 minutes. Keep an eye on them!

- Once they're nice and browned on all sides, place them in a deep mixing bowl and pour your prepared hot sauce over them. Toss to coat them evenly.

Mushroom, Spinach, and Sausage Crustless Quiche

- 1/2 teaspoon salt

- 1/4 teaspoon fresh black pepper

- 8 eggs

- 1/3 cup coconut milk (low-fat or full fat)

- 2 Tablespoon butter, bacon grease, or olive oil

- 10 oz baby bella mushrooms, sliced

- 1/2 teaspoon dried thyme

- 1 spicy Italian chicken sausage diced

- 1 package of fresh spinach (or kale) (3 to 4 cups)

DIRECTIONS

- Preheat oven to 375 F. Butter a 9-inch pie pan or cake pan and set aside.

- In a medium bowl, whisk eggs, salt, pepper, and coconut milk. Set aside.

- In a heavy skillet, heat butter over medium heat. Add mushrooms and thyme in a single layer and sauté until browned. Don't crowd them. Toss in sausage and brown (about 2 minutes) stirring often. Add spinach on top of cooked mushrooms and sausage. Stir and cook until spinach is slightly wilted, about 1 to 2 minutes. Remove skillet from heat. Add a pinch of salt and pepper to taste.

- Spoon and spread the mushroom, sausage, and spinach evenly into the prepared pie pan. Top this with the egg mixture.

- Bake for 35 to 40 minutes, or until slightly golden brown on edges, puffed and set in the middle. Serve warm or at room temperature. Leftovers are great reheated for breakfast or lunch.

Tuna Quinoa Salad in Endive Wraps

- 1/4 cup quinoa cooked

- 1 can tuna in water

- 1/4 cup plain Greek Yogurt nonfat

- 1 tsp. lemon juice

- 2 tbsp. radish diced

- 2 tbsp. parsley dried

- 1/2 tsp. fresh dill

- salt & pepper to taste

- endive leaves to make wraps

DIRECTIONS

- In a bowl, add all ingredients and stir to combine.

- Transfer to a meal prep container and add endive leaves. The more, the better!

- Chill in the refrigerator a minimum of 20 minutes before eating for the flavours to marry.

Slow-Cooker Vegetable Soup

- 1 medium onion, chopped

- 2 medium carrots chopped

- 2 stalks celery, chopped

- 12 ounces fresh green beans cut into ½-inch pieces

- 4 cups chopped kale

- 2 medium zucchini chopped

- 4 Roma tomatoes, seeded and chopped

- 2 cloves garlic, minced

- 2 (15 ounces) cans no-salt-added cannellini or other white beans, rinsed

- 4 cups low-sodium chicken broth or low-sodium vegetable broth

- 2 teaspoons salt

- ½ teaspoon ground pepper

- 2 teaspoons red-wine vinegar

- 8 teaspoons prepared pesto

DIRECTIONS

- Combine onion, carrots, celery, green beans, kale, zucchini, tomatoes, garlic, white beans, broth, salt, and pepper in a 6-quart or larger slow cooker. Cook on High for 4 hours or Low for 6 hours. Stir in vinegar and top each serving of soup with 1 teaspoon pesto.

Cauliflower Rice Stuffed Peppers

- Cauliflower rice:

- 1 medium head cauliflower grated into 'rice' (see method here)

- 1 Tbsp olive or grapeseed oil

- 3 cloves garlic, minced (optional)

- 1 cup diced red, white, yellow, or green onion (I recommend red)

- 1 pinch each sea salt and black pepper

- Peppers:

- 4 large red, yellow, or orange bell peppers (halved seeds removed)

- 1 15-ounce can black or pinto beans (rinsed and drained // if unsalted, add additional salt to taste)

- 2/3 cup salsa (plus more for serving // very flavorful salsa, like Trader Joe's Chunky Salsa)

- 2 tsp cumin powder (plus more to taste)

- 2 tsp chili powder (plus more to taste)

- 2-3 Tbsp lime juice

- 1/4 tsp each sea salt and black pepper (plus more to taste)

- Optional toppings:

- 1 medium ripe avocado (sliced)

- Fresh lime juice

- Hot sauce

- Cilantro, chopped

- Diced red onion

- Creamy Cilantro Dressing

- Chipotle Red Salsa (or your favorite salsa)

DIRECTIONS

- Preheat oven to 375 degrees F (190 C) and set out a 9x13-inch baking dish or rimmed baking sheet. Also, brush halved peppers with a neutral, high heat oil, such as grape seed, avocado, or refined coconut. Set aside.

- Prepare cauliflower rice by following these instructions. Then heat a large rimmed skillet over medium heat.

- Once hot, add oil, garlic (optional), onion, salt, and pepper. Sauté for 1 minute, stirring frequently. Then add cauliflower 'rice' and stir to coat. Place the lid on to steam the rice for about 1 minute. Then remove from heat and transfer the mixture to a large mixing bowl. You aren't looking to thoroughly cook the 'rice,' as it will continue cooking in the oven.

- Add remaining ingredients - black beans through salt and pepper - to the cauliflower rice and mix to combine thoroughly. Taste and adjust seasonings accordingly, adding salt, pepper, or more spices as desired.

- Generously stuff halved peppers with ~ 1/2 cup of the mixture until all peppers are full (you may have a little leftover filling, which can be added to salads or served on the side), then cover the dish with foil.

- Bake for 30 minutes covered. Then remove foil, increase heat to 400 degrees F (204 C), and bake for another 15-20 minutes or until peppers are soft and slightly golden brown. For softer peppers, bake 5-10 minutes more. Serve with desired toppings (listed above) or as is. I recommend avocado, lime juice, hot sauce, and cilantro.

- Best when fresh, though leftovers keep covered in the refrigerator for 2-3 days. Reheat in a 350 degree F (176 C) oven until warmed through - about 20 minutes. See notes for instructions on making ahead of time.

Dinner Recipes

Sheet Pan Chicken with Sweet Potatoes Apples and Brussels Sprouts

- 4 boneless skinless chicken breasts, — trimmed of excess fat and lightly pounded to a relatively even thickness

- 3 tablespoons extra-virgin olive oil — divided

- 4 cloves garlic — minced

- 2 tablespoons chopped fresh rosemary — divided

- 1 teaspoon ground cinnamon

- 1 teaspoon kosher salt — divided

- 1/2 teaspoon black pepper — divided

- 4 cups Brussels sprouts — trimmed and halved (quarter if huge), about 1 pound

- 1 large sweet potato — peeled and cut into 1/2-inch cubes

- 1 medium red onion — cut into 3/4-inch pieces

- 1 medium Granny Smith apple — peeled, cored, and cut into rough 1-inch pieces (these pieces should be larger than the other vegetables)

DIRECTIONS

- Preheat the oven to 425 degrees F.

- Place the chicken breasts in a large ziptop bag. Drizzle with 1 1/2 tablespoons olive oil, then add the garlic, 1 tablespoon rosemary, cinnamon, 1/2 teaspoon salt, and 1/4 teaspoon black pepper. Zip the bag tightly, then shake and rub the bag to coat the chicken in the oil and spices. Set aside while you chop the vegetables and apples, or refrigerate for up to 1 day.

- Once chopped, place the Brussels sprouts, sweet potato, onion, and apple on a large, rimmed baking sheet. Drizzle with the remaining 1 1/2 tablespoons olive oil, then sprinkle with remaining 1/2 teaspoon kosher salt and 1/4 teaspoon black pepper. Toss to evenly coat, then spread into an even layer.

- Remove the chicken from the marinade and place it on top of the apple and vegetables. Place in the oven and roast until the chicken is cooked through and the internal temperature reaches 160 to 165 degrees F, about 18 to 22 minutes, or until done. Once the chicken is cooked through, remove to a plate to rest and cover with foil to keep warm. Toss the apple and vegetables on the pan, then return the pan to the oven and continue baking until caramelized and tender, about 10 to 15 additional minutes. Sprinkle with the remaining 1 tablespoon fresh rosemary. Serve warm with the rested chicken.

Greek-Spiced Lamb Roast

- 1 onion, large, cut into slices and separated

- 1 red potato, large, cut into 1" cubes

- 6 cloves garlic, smashed and roughly diced

- 2-3 tbsp Kasandrinos olive oil

- 3 tbsp Balanced Bites Greek Blend, divided (1 tbsp for veggies, 1 tbsp each for the top-side and bottom-side of the meat)

- 1.5 lb lamb top sirloin roast

DIRECTIONS

- Preheat oven to 375°F.

- Add all veggies to 12" cast iron skillet. Drizzle veggies with 2-3 tbsp olive oil - sprinkle about 1 tbsp Greek blend over vegetables. Stir to coat veggies in oil and spices.

- On cutting board, sprinkle about 1 tbsp Greek blend on bottom-side of meat; pat down to make sure the spices stick. Place roast in the center of the skillet with seasoning side down. Season the top-side of the meat, pat down to make sure the spices stick.

- Insert an oven-safe digital meat thermometer with a probe into the center of the roast, and set for 160°F. Bake at 375°F until the meat thermometer goes off! (approximately 45-60 minutes for a 1.5 lb roast)

6-Minute Salmon

- 2 wild salmon filets

- 2 pinches of sea salt

- 1 teaspoon SAVORY Balanced Bites spice blend, divided between the filets. An essential starting point would be sea salt, black pepper, and garlic powder and finish with freshly squeezed lemon when serving.

DIRECTIONS

- Preheat a cast-iron skillet to high heat and set your toaster oven or oven to the broiler setting.

- Take the filet of salmon and pat dry with a paper towel. Salt the skin side of the salmon and add it to the pan, skin side down. Set the timer for two minutes. While the skin side is searing, season the other side generously with the SAVORY spice blend.

- Once the salmon is seared, place the cast iron pan into the toaster oven or oven for 4 minutes under the broiler.

- That's it! Once the 4 minutes are up, the salmon will be perfectly cooked and ready to be served.

Chimichurri Chicken Green Beans Skillet

For the green beans:

- 4 cups green beans — ends chopped off

- 1 tablespoon olive oil

- 2 garlic cloves — fine sliced

- Salt & black pepper to taste

- For the Chimichurri sauce:

- 1 cup parsley—you can also use cilantro instead

- ¼ cup red onion—chopped

- 1/2 teaspoon salt—or to taste

- ¼ teaspoon pepper—or to taste

- 2 garlic cloves

- ½ teaspoon dried oregano

- ⅓ cup + 1 tablespoon olive oil

- 1 teaspoon lemon juice

- 2 tablespoons red wine vinegar

- For the chicken:

- 1 tbsp olive oil

- 2 medium skinless free-range organic chicken breast

- Salt and ground black pepper to taste

- Paprika to taste

DIRECTIONS

- Bring a pot of water to a boil. Add green beans and allow boiling for 4-5 minutes.

- Drain green beans and set aside.

- In a skillet, heat the olive oil on medium heat.

- Add garlic and cook for 30 to 60 seconds. Add green beans and cook for 3-5 minutes.

- Season with salt & pepper. Set aside. While you are cooking the green beans, make the chimichurri sauce. See the instructions below.

- Add all the Chimichurri ingredients in a food processor and process on low. For about 1-3 minutes. Let it rest for about 20 minutes.

- Season it chicken with salt, pepper, and paprika.

- Place chicken on a greased skillet and cook over medium heat for 3-4 minutes on each side or until the chicken is cooked through.

- Pour the Chimichurri sauce over it and bring the green beans back to the skillet. Enjoy!

Ginger Sesame Zucchini Noodles with Shrimp

- 1 Tablespoon avocado oil or olive oil

- 1/2 pound medium raw shrimp

- 2 Tablespoons coconut aminos

- 2 Tablespoons sesame oil

- 1-inch piece of fresh ginger, peeled and grated

- 2 cloves garlic, grated

- 2 green onions, thinly sliced

- 1 Tablespoon sesame seeds

- 1 pound zucchini, spiralized

DIRECTIONS

- Heat the oil in a large skillet set over high heat. Add the shrimp and cook 4-5 minutes, or until bright pink and cooked through.

- While the shrimp cook, combine the coconut aminos, sesame oil, ginger, garlic, green onions, and sesame seeds in a large bowl. Add the zucchini noodles and toss to coat.

- Divide the zucchini noodles between two plates. Top with shrimp.

Carrot Meatballs with Mint Cauliflower Rice

For the Meatballs:

- 1 lb. lean ground beef, chicken or turkey
- 1 large egg
- ½ cup grated carrots
- 1 tsp. Italian seasoning
- ½ tsp. crushed red pepper flakes
- salt & pepper to taste
- 2 tbsp. extra virgin olive oil
- For the Cauliflower Rice:
- 4 cups diced cauliflower
- 1 tbsp. lemon juice
- 4 mint leaves

- salt & pepper to taste

- ½ cup of water

DIRECTIONS

- In a large bowl, whisk together the egg with Italian seasoning, salt, pepper, and red pepper flakes.

- Add carrots and ground meat to the bowl. Using your hands, mix the ingredients thoroughly throughout the meat. Using a small ice cream scoop, roll the meat into balls until 18 meatballs are made, and the meat is gone.

- Heat a medium skillet over medium-high heat. Add oil to the pan and heat 4 minutes, then add the meatballs to the pan.

- Cook meatballs 5 minutes then flip to cook on the other side another 5 minutes. Rotate the meatballs a few more times in the pan cooking 1-2 minutes until cooked through. Remove meatballs from the pan and place on a plate.

- Add ¼ cup water to the skillet with riced cauliflower. Cook 5 minutes until softened, then add lemon juice and mint leaves. Stir to combine.

- Divide the meatballs and cauliflower rice into 4 even servings, placing them in meal prep containers with fresh lemon wedges.

No-Cook Black Bean Salad

- ½ cup thinly sliced red onion

- 1 medium ripe avocado, pitted and roughly chopped

- ¼ cup cilantro leaves

- ¼ cup lime juice2 tablespoons extra-virgin olive oil1 clove garlic, minced

- ½ teaspoon salt

- 8 cups mixed salad greens

- 2 medium ears corn, kernels removed, or 2 cups frozen corn, thawed and patted dry

- 1-pint grape tomatoes halved

- 1 (15 ounces) can black beans, rinsed

DIRECTIONS

- Place onion in a medium bowl and cover with cold water. Set aside. Combine avocado, cilantro, lime juice, oil, garlic, and salt in a mini food processor. Process, scraping down the sides as needed, until smooth and creamy. Just before serving, combine salad greens, corn, tomatoes, and beans in a large bowl. Drain the onions and add to the bowl, along with the avocado dressing. Toss to coat.

Bang Bang Shrimp Lettuce Wraps

- 1 lb. peeled, deveined and tail-off Shrimp

- 1-2 tbsp. cooking oil (I used avocado oil)

- salt and pepper, to taste

- For the sauce:

- 1/2 cup homemade or primal kitchens mayo

- 2 cloves garlic, minced

- 2 tsp. mina harissa

- 1 tsp. fish sauce

- 2 tsp. fresh lime juice

- salt and pepper, to taste

- For serving:

- 1/4 cup sliced scallions (green part only)

- 1/4 cup fresh cilantro leaves (or cilantro microgreens)

- 6-8 butter lettuce leaves

DIRECTIONS

- Combine all of the bang-bang sauce ingredients in a bowl and set aside until ready to use.

- Pat, the shrimp dry and season with salt and pepper, to taste.

- Heat a large skillet over medium-high heat. Brush oil so that it evenly coats the bottom of the skillet.

- Spread the shrimp in a single layer across the skillet without overcrowding the pan (I had to do mine in two separate batches). Sear both sides of the shrimp until a light, golden crust forms (about 3-4 minutes per side).

- Remove the shrimp from the heat but still keep them in the hot skillet. Spoon the desired amount of bang bang sauce into the skillet and toss to coat the shrimp.

- Serve in lettuce cups topped with scallions and cilantro.

SNACKS

Hungry between meals and need something to lunch on? Sugar cleanse-friendly snacks include fruits and vegetables (excluding starches). You can add sugar-free dipping sauces or mix it up with a cup of unsweetened yogurt and some nuts. If you're looking for something that reminds you of processed foods, take a look at the recipes below.

Toasted Pine Nut Herb Pumpkin Muffins

- 1 cup cashew meal

- 1/4 cup tapioca flour/starch

- 2 tablespoons coconut flour

- 1/2 tablespoon baking powder

- 1/2 teaspoon kosher salt

- 1/4 teaspoon freshly ground black pepper

- 1/4 cup toasted pine nuts

- 3 eggs

- 1 cup pumpkin puree

- 1 tablespoon chopped rosemary

- 1 tablespoon chopped sage

DIRECTIONS

- Preheat oven to 350 degrees. Grease a muffin tin with baking spray.

- Combine the flours, baking powder, salt, pepper, and 2/3 of the toasted pine nuts in a large bowl.

- Whisk together the remaining ingredients in a medium bowl.

- Add the wet to the dry and mix until thoroughly combined.

- Scoop the batter into the muffin tins and top with the remaining toasted pine nuts.

- Bake for 18-20 minutes until set.

- Remove from oven, let cool 3-5 minutes in the pan before running a knife around the muffins and popping them out onto a cooling rack.

Granny Smith Apple Crumble

- For the filling:

- 4 green apples, peeled and thinly sliced

- juice of 1/2 lemon

- 1 teaspoon ground cinnamon

- For the topping:

- 1 1/4 cups almond meal or other nut meal of your choice, store-bought or homemade

- 1/4 cup unsalted butter or coconut oil, softened

- 1 teaspoon ground cinnamon

- pinch of sea salt

- 1 tablespoon unsalted butter or coconut oil, melted, for the pan

DIRECTIONS

- Preheat the oven to 350 °F.

- Make the filling: In a mixing bowl, toss the apples with the lemon juice and cinnamon.

- Make the topping: In a separate bowl, mix together the almond meal, butter or coconut oil, cinnamon, and salt until completely incorporated.

- Brush the bottom and sides of a 9 by 9-inch or similar-sized baking dish with the melted butter or coconut oil.

- Place the apples in the baking dish and cover evenly with the topping.

- Bake for 20 minutes covered with foil, then for an additional 25 to 30 minutes uncovered, until the apples are soft and the topping begins to brown on the edges.

Vanilla "Milkshake"

- 1 cup frozen riced cauliflower

- ½-1 cup unsweetened canned coconut milk (adjust the amount of liquid to blend into a smooth, thick "milkshake" consistency)

- ½ cup chilled brewed vanilla tea (optional)

- ½ tsp. vanilla extract (or seeds from vanilla bean pod)

- 1-2 scoops collagen peptides

- Additional ice (optional)

DIRECTIONS

- Combine all ingredients in a small nutri-bullet or blender and blend until thick, smooth, and creamy.

Baked Eggplant Fries with Goat Cheese Dip

For the eggplant fries:

- 1 medium or 2 small eggplants (preferably the less bitter Japanese variety)

- 2 Tablespoons/16g arrowroot flour

- 1 cup/112g almond flour

- 1/2 teaspoon sea salt

- 1/2 teaspoon ground coriander seed

- 1/2 teaspoon ground cumin seed

- 1/8 to 1/4 teaspoon cayenne pepper (depending on how spicy you want it)

- 1 Tablespoon of organic coconut oil or extra-virgin olive oil

- 1 large egg

- For the goat cheese dipping sauce:

- 4 ounces/113g goat cheese

- 1/4 cup/ 60ml goat milk or goat milk kefir (or regular milk if you can't find goat milk)

- the juice of half a lemon

- 1/4 teaspoon sea salt

- Freshly ground black pepper

DIRECTIONS

- Blend goat cheese, milk, lemon juice, salt, and a pinch of pepper in a food processor until smooth and creamy.

- Transfer dip to a serving bowl. Serve with baked eggplant fries.

- Dip can be made ahead and refrigerated, bring to room temperature before serving.

- Preheat oven to 425 degrees F. Line a baking sheet with lightly greased parchment paper.

- Cut the eggplant in half then into thin slices lengthwise and cut those into batons about the size of French fries.

- Stir together the arrowroot flour almond flour and salt and divide evenly onto two shallow plates.

- In a separate bowl, whisk together the coriander, cumin, and cayenne pepper with the coconut oil and egg.

- Roll the eggplant fries into the almond flour mixture on the first plate, then quickly dip into the egg mixture and then into the second plate of almond flour.

- Place the eggplant fries evenly onto the baking sheet and sprinkle with an extra pinch of sea salt.

- Bake it for 15 to-20 minutes(depending on how thick your fries are) or until crispy and browned. Serve with goat cheese dipping sauce.

Savoury Almond Crackers

- 1 cup almond meal

- 3 Tbsp. coconut flour

- 1 heaped Tbsp. almond butter

- 1 egg (or ½ Tbsp. flax meal mixed in 2 Tbsp. water for egg-free option)

- ¼ – ½ tsp. sea salt

- Cracked black pepper (optional)

- Add-ins:

- ½ cup sundried tomatoes packed in olive oil, drained and chopped

- 2-4 cloves roasted garlic

- 2 Tbsp. chopped fresh herbs (basil, rosemary, thyme – individual or a combination)

- ½ cup Kalamata olives, pit removed and chopped

- ½ cup roasted peppers, chopped

DIRECTIONS

- Preheat oven to 350 °F.

- Line a tray with baking paper.

- Place the almond meal and coconut flour into a bowl and mix to combine.

- Add the almond butter and egg (or substitute) and stir to combine.

- Add your choice of add-ins, salt, and pepper (if using).

- Work the mixture into a dough and shape into a smooth ball (hands work best).

- Place the dough between two sheets of baking paper and roll with a rolling pin until the mixture is approximately 1/4" thick.

- Place the dough onto your prepared tray and score into squares.

- Bake for ten minutes, turning the tray halfway through cooking.

- Remove the crackers from the oven and allow to cool slightly.

- Break the crackers along the scored lines and turn them around on the tray so that the outer pieces are now on the inside and return to the oven for a further 10 minutes.

- Remove the crackers from the oven and allow to cool on the tray for 5 minutes before gently moving to a cooling rack.

- Store in an airtight container.

No-Bake Chocolate Banana Bites

For the batter:

- 2 green-tipped bananas

- 3 Tbsp. coconut oil

- 1 ½ Tbsp. cocoa powder

- 3 Tbsp. cashew nut butter (other nut kinds of butter can be substituted)

- 1 Tbsp. cassava flour

- For rolling:

- 2-3 Tbsp. shredded coconut (unsweetened)

- 2-3 Tbsp. chopped pecans (or other nuts)

DIRECTIONS

- Add all ingredients (except shredded coconut and chopped pecans) to a food processor. Pulse until well combined.

- Refrigerate for 15 minutes to firm up the batter.

- On a cutting board, evenly distribute the shredded coconut and the chopped pecans for rolling.

- Using a spoon or cookie dough scoop, roll the batter into balls and roll the balls onto the shredded coconut and pecan mixture until well coated.

- Refrigerate for 45 minutes (or freeze for 20 minutes) to firm up the batter. Take the balls out of the refrigerator about 15 minutes before serving,

Salt and Vinegar Popcorn Cauliflower

- 1 large head cauliflower, broken into small florets
- 3/4 cup Nakano original seasoned rice vinegar
- 1/4 cup blanched almond flour
- 1/4 cup tapioca flour
- 1 tablespoon coconut flour
- salt and pepper

DIRECTIONS

- Preheat oven to 425 degrees and line a baking sheet with parchment paper.
- Place cauliflower florets in a large bowl. Pour the vinegar over the cauliflower and toss to combine. Set aside and let marinate for 15-20 minutes.
- Combine flours, salt, and pepper in a large storage container or ziplock bag.

- Using a slotted spoon, remove cauliflower, draining excess vinegar, and place in the container with the flour mixture. Cover or close container/bag and shake until all the florets are coated with the mixture.

- Spread the cauliflower out onto the baking sheet in an even layer.

- Bake for 20 minutes, flip gently using a large spatula and continue baking for another 20-25 minutes until crispy and golden brown.

- Remove from the oven and serve warm.

Garlic Aioli and Kale Chips

For the kale chips:

- 1 bunch of kale

- Olive oil, for drizzling

- Salt and pepper, to taste

- For the garlic aioli:

- 1 egg yolk, at room temperature

- 2 Tablespoons lemon juice

- 1/2 teaspoon mustard powder

- 1/2 cup avocado oil

- 1/2 cup olive oil

- 2-3 garlic cloves

- 2-3 sprigs of rosemary

DIRECTIONS

- Preheat your oven to 275 F.

- Wash the kale well and remove the leaves from the stems.

- Place the leaves on a cookie sheet. Drizzle olive oil and sprinkle salt and pepper to taste.

- Place in the oven for 20 minutes. In the meantime, make the aioli.

- Place the egg, lemon juice, and mustard powder in a food processor or blender. Blend or pulse until frothy (2-3 pulses).

- This is an important step. Take your time, or you will mess up the recipe. I put the avocado and olive oil in the same bowl after measuring. Slowly add the oil mixture tablespoon by tablespoon while the blender or food processor is on. Once you have added about 1/3-1/2 cup of the oil, you can pour it in quicker. This step should take 2-3 minutes. I use the small hole feature on top of the food processor.

- Now you should have mayo. Add the garlic and rosemary into the blender or food processor and pulse until combined well.

- Serve with chips for dipping!

Sugar Detox Tips and Tricks

Know what kind of person you are. Some people benefit from cutting down on sugar slowly. Others see more success from going cold turkey on sugar. You know yourself best. It's up to you to decide which way you will best succeed. If you intend to cut down slowly, begin by replacing snacks with noninflammatory options. Then return your meals one at a time. If you want to go cold turkey, it will help to clear your pantry of sugary foods before you begin so that its harder to give in to cravings when they strike.

Plan meals and do your shopping in advance. Make a list of ingredients you need for the week's meals and brine that with you when you shop. You're less likely to give in to temptations if you buy according to a list. Only go down the aisles you need food from, and avoid walking down the snacks aisles.

Meal prep beforehand. At the beginning of the week, after planning meals and shopping, do as much meal prep as possible. You can cook meals and store them in the fridge and freezer for when you want to eat them, or you can prep ingredients. Chop up vegetables, marinate your meats, and mix your spices to make it quicker and easier to cook each day.

Don't shop hungry. Shopping while hungry can lead to impulse buys that fill your pantry and your stomach with the same sugars you're trying to get rid of. The fix is simple: shop after healthy, filling meals.

Eat a hearty breakfast. It's important to begin the day with a protein-packed breakfast. Focus on making time to prepare a healthy breakfast. Starting the day with a healthy meal sets your day up for success, whereas eating a sugary breakfast starts your day with a roller coaster of blood sugar changes—not a good start to the day.

Manage your stress properly. Stress and other negative emotions can cause cravings, and if you're stressed, you'll be more likely to give in to those cravings. If you have trouble managing your stress, be sure to exercise and take time to relax and destress daily.

Sleep well. Sleep deprivation can also cause cravings. Practice good sleep hygiene: have a consistent sleep routine, avoid alcohol and caffeine before sleep, turn off technology an hour before bed, and establish a bedtime routine. It's essential to get enough quality sleep each night, not just during a sugar detox.

Do not skip meals. Your body will be under stress as it adjusts to a lower sugar diet. Skipping meals will cause a drop in your blood sugar, leaving you craving sugar and carbs to bring it back up.

Hold yourself accountable. If it helps you stay on track, establish rewards for your successes. Celebrate five days without sugar by seeing a movie (no popcorn) or taking a hike someplace new. You know what system will work best to keep you on track. Use it. Take full advantage of it. Whether it's daily reminders from a friend or a personal promise to buy that new piece of clothing you've had your eye on when you succeed, use it. Changing habits is hard. You want to set yourself up for success. But...

Don't beat yourself up for mistakes. One mistake doesn't mean you should quit your detox. When you mess up, the best thing for you to do is to keep trying. Continue to work towards eating a sugar-free diet and accept that you messed up. If Thomas Edison had given up the first time he messed up, we wouldn't have electric lights (well, actually that's up for debate, but you get the point).

Healthy on a budget. Healthy eating seems expensive, but there are ways to counteract that and make it much more affordable. Buy brand name products instead of name brand products. They're often the same or very similar, just with different packaging. Buy from bulk bins. If your supermarket has bulk bins, check to see if the cost per unit is less than buying a bag or box, and if it is, start buying from there. Even if the bulk bins aren't cheaper per unit, if you only intend to use a small amount, the total cost may end up being less from the bulk bins. Frozen vegetables are often cheaper than fresh vegetables, and they tend to be healthier since they're frozen soon after being picked. Buy produce that's in season, and don't buy it when it's offseason.

Invest in freezer-safe containers. Having something to put your leftovers and extra foods will save you from having to throw away and repurchase foods. Make sure you know the best ways to store your produce to keep it fresh longer.

Protein for cheap. Meat is expensive. It helps to buy large packs when the meat goes on sale and freeze what you won't use soon. Have more days with meatless meals and replace the protein from meat with beans and lentils.

Don't be afraid to shop at different stores. Depending on where you live, you may have access to ethnic supermarkets, where certain products may be cheaper. Figure out which days foods go on sale and hunt around for coupons to save a little bit extra.

If you're baking, place one part sugar with one part unsweetened applesauce for an easy switch to a sugar-free recipe.

Above all, do what helps you. Identify the patterns and routines that make it most comfortable for you to manage and build on those to establish healthy eating and lifestyle habits.

Conclusion

We've established that sugars are harmful both for our health and for the environment, and we've discussed what to do about it. Sugary foods cause health problems ranging from cavities to obesity and may even play a role in the development of cancer and Alzheimer's disease. Sugars sap our energy and make our blood sugar unstable. They take a high toll on the environment, too. A high price to pay for sweets.

The solution to this is to commit to a low-sugar diet starting with our 30-day sugar detox plan. Commit to living sugar-free for 30 days, and you'll experience higher energy levels, more magnificent immune functioning, and even improved mood. Despite cravings and a brief period of withdrawal, you'll notice significant improvements in your quality of life mentally and physically.

By planning, you can set yourself up for success in cutting out sugar. Create meal plans, restock your pantry with healthy foods, and gather support from the people around you to start your detox off on the right foot.

You now know the facts. You know what sugar does to your body and your mind. What will you do about it? Will you continue to let sugar eat away at your life? Or will you take the reins and make the changes you need to live a long healthy life?

FINAL WORDS

Thank you again for purchasing this book!

We hope this book can help you.

The next step is for you to **join our email newsletter** to receive updates on any upcoming new book releases or promotions. You can sign up for free, and as a bonus, you will also receive our "*7 Fitness Mistakes You Don't Know You're Making*" book! This bonus book breaks down many of the most common fitness mistakes and will demystify many of the complexities and science of getting into shape. Having all this fitness knowledge and science organized into an actionable step-by-step book will help you get started in the right direction in your fitness journey! To join our free email newsletter and grab your free book, please visit the link and sign up: **www.effingopublishing.com/gift**

Finally, if you enjoyed this book, then we would like to ask you for a favor, would you be kind enough to leave a review for this book? It would be much appreciated! Thank you, and good luck with your journey!

About the Co-Author

Our name is Alex & George Kaplo; we're both certified personal trainers from Montreal, Canada. We will start by saying we are not the biggest guys you will ever meet, and this has never really been our goal. We started working out to overcome our biggest insecurity when we were younger, which was our self-confidence. You may be going through some challenges right now, or you may want to get fit, and we can certainly relate.

We always kind were interested in the health & fitness world and wanted to gain some muscle due to the numerous bullying in our teenage years. We figured we could do something about what our body looks like. This was the beginning of our transformation journey. We had no idea where to start, but we both just got started. We felt worried and afraid at times that other people would make fun of us for doing the exercises the wrong way. We always wished we had a friend to guide us and who could show us the ropes.

After a lot of work, studying, and countless trials and errors. Some people began to notice how we were both getting more fit and how we were starting to form a keen interest in the topic. This led many friends and new faces to come to us and ask us for fitness advice. At first, it seemed odd when people asked us to help them get in shape. But what kept us going is when they started to see changes in their own body and told us it's the first time that they saw real results! From there, more people kept coming to us, and it made both of us realize after so much reading and studying in this field that it did help us, but it also allowed us to help others. To date, we have coached and trained numerous clients who have achieved some pretty amazing results.

Today, both of us own & operate this publishing business, where we bring passionate and expert authors to write about health and fitness topics. We also run an online fitness business, and we would love to connect with you by inviting you to visit the website on the following page and signing up for our e-mail newsletter (you will even get a free book).

Last but not least, if you are in the position we were once in and you want some guidance, don't hesitate and ask... I will be there to help you out!

Your coaches,

Alex & George Kaplo

Download another book for Free

We want to thank you for purchasing this book and offer you another book (just as long and valuable as this book), "Health & Fitness Mistakes You Don't Know You're Making," completely free.

Visit the link below to sign up and receive it:

www.effingopublishing.com/gift

In this book, we will break down the most common health & fitness mistakes, you are probably committing right now, and will reveal how you can quickly get in the best shape of your life!

In addition to this valuable gift, you will also have an opportunity to get our new books for free, enter giveaways, and receive other useful emails from us. Again, visit the link to sign up:

www.effingopublishing.com/gift

Copyright 2019 by Effingo Publishing - All Rights Reserved.

This document by Effingo Publishing, owned by the A&G Direct Inc company, is geared towards providing exact and reliable information in regards to the topic and issue covered. The publication is sold with the idea that the publisher is not required to render accounting, officially permitted or otherwise qualified services. If advice is necessary, legal or professional, a practiced individual in the profession should be ordered.

From a Declaration of Principles which was accepted and approved equally by a Committee of the American Bar Association and a Committee of Publishers and Associations.

In no way is it legal to reproduce, duplicate, or transmit any part of this document in either electronic means or printed format. Recording of this publication is strictly prohibited, and any storage of this document is not allowed unless with written permission from the publisher. All rights reserved.

The information provided herein is stated to be truthful and consistent, in that any liability, in terms of inattention or otherwise, by any usage or abuse of any policies, processes, or directions contained within is the solitary and utter responsibility of the recipient reader. Under no circumstances will any legal obligation or blame be held against the publisher for any reparation, damages, or monetary loss due to the information herein, either directly or indirectly.

The information herein is offered for informational purposes solely and is universal as so. The presentation of the information is without a contract or any guarantee assurance.

The trademarks that are used are without any consent, and the publication of the trademark is without permission or backing by the trademark owner. All trademarks and brands within this book are for clarifying purposes only and are owned by the owners themselves, not affiliated with this document.

For more great books, visit:
EffingoPublishing.com

www.ingramcontent.com/pod-product-compliance
Lightning Source LLC
Chambersburg PA
CBHW070913080526
44589CB00013B/1274